HISTORY & GEOGRAPHY 1204
HISTORY OF GOVERNMENTS

INTRODUCTION |3

1. ANCIENT GOVERNMENTS 5

A PRIMITIVE GOVERNMENT PRIMER |6
BEGINNING OF DEMOCRACY |9
ANCIENT ROMAN GOVERNMENT |11
SELF TEST 1 |15

2. GOVERNMENTAL SYSTEMS 19

FEUDALISM |20
THEOCRACY |24
DEMOCRACY |27
SELF TEST 2 |31

3. DICTATORSHIP 34

FASCISM |34
NAZISM |38
SELF TEST 3 |41

LIFEPAC Test is located in the center of the booklet. Please remove before starting the unit.

Author:
Brad Zockoll

Editor:
Brian Ring

Media Credits:
Page 9: © PanosKarapanagiotis, iStock, Thinkstock; **21:** © heywoody, iStock, Thinkstock; **25:** © BibleArt-Library, iStock, Thinkstock; **27:** © giftlegacy, iStock, Thinkstock; **28:** © Zoonar/S.Heap, Zoonar, Thinkstock; © emarto, iStock, Thinkstock; © Lobro78, iStock, Thinkstock; © KathyKafka, iStock, Thinkstock; **35, 38:** © Photos.com, Thinkstock.

Alpha Omega
PUBLICATIONS

804 N. 2nd Ave. E.
Rock Rapids, IA 51246-1759

History of Governments

Introduction

What is needed to establish a government? A group of settlers arrive in a new land teeming with fish, game, and forests. There are natural resources in abundance, and there is no doubt that this is the place to start a new colony. But where do you go from here? Who sets up the government? Should the society be democratic or socialist? What ingredients make up a good government? If you were to establish a colony, what principles would you need to know? By examining the many forms of government that were established by tribes and nations, we can gain an idea for some of the building blocks required to make a government successful. There are simple foundational truths that are consistent with almost any government—good or bad—that help organize and strengthen the structure.

Objectives

Read these objectives. The objectives tell you what you will be able to do when you have successfully completed this LIFEPAC®. When you have finished this LIFEPAC, you should be able to:

1. Describe the elements necessary for a successful and effective government.

2. Explain the history and direction of democracy in ancient Greece and Athens.

3. Explain the concept of a "republic" and be able to compare and contrast Roman and Greek forms of government.

4. Explain the concept of "feudalism" and its effect on people in the Middle Ages.

5. Describe a theocracy.

6. Describe a democracy.

7. Describe fascism and give examples from history of fascist leaders and countries.

8. Describe and give a brief history of Nazism.

Survey the LIFEPAC. Ask yourself some questions about this study and write your questions here.

_____

_____

_____

_____

_____

_____

_____

_____

_____

_____

_____

_____

1. ANCIENT GOVERNMENTS

Section Objectives

Review these objectives. When you have completed this section, you should be able to:

1. Describe the elements necessary for a successful and effective government.
2. Explain the history and direction of democracy in ancient Greece and Athens.
3. Explain the concept of a "republic" and be able to compare and contrast Roman and Greek forms of government.

Vocabulary

Study these words to enhance your learning success in this section.

colony	A group of people settled in a particular area who carry the same interests.
decimated	To reduce the amount in blocks or sizeable amounts.
democratic	Relating to a government or organized group that strives to be fair and equal to all people.
natural resources	Available supply of goods made possible by God's creation; not man-made.
production	The making of goods that can be used or worn for protection or well-being.
settler	An emigrant who has arrived in a new area to create a home.
socialist	A form of government where goods and services and the political power are distributed among the people.
sustenance	Food and drink; necessary foods in order to stay alive.

Note: *All vocabulary words in this LIFEPAC appear in* **boldface** *print the first time they are used. If you are not sure of the meaning when you are reading, study the definitions given.*

A PRIMITIVE GOVERNMENT PRIMER

What is needed to establish a government?

1. Leadership is needed. Whether they want to be governed by a group of leaders or a solitary decision-maker, any group of people who want to establish themselves in an orderly manner must have leadership. The Bible shows us many examples of leaders who took their responsibility seriously, through good and bad times. Moses, Aaron, and David are just a few of the leaders who were able to enhance the growth of their governments by being the proper point of authority. Any government needs a leader to whom the people can turn. There must be a stopping place in the decision-making process where the population can feel satisfied that someone is taking responsibility. As many organizations will say, "The buck stops here!" Who is in charge? Whether it is a monarchy, democracy or even oligarchy, there must be a final point of authority. Sam Houston of the **Republic** of Texas is a fine example of a leader who kept a government strong and active.

2. Safety is a priority. Measures must be taken to be safe. Think of it—who would want to be part of an organization that could not assure a secure surrounding? People settling in an area want to feel safe from outside attacks. What if an enemy creeps in and tries to destroy the group? Protection might not be in the form of a **standing army** or a powerful navy, but any population that seeks to be independent needs to have a guarantee that the citizens could be free from damage or danger. A good government needs to organize a group that would ensure its protection. Founded in the wilderness, areas such as Fort Pitt (which would later become the city of Pittsburgh) made safety one of their top priorities.

3. Production and sustenance should be provided daily. Food is needed for people to live. People need to eat, and they must be given the opportunity to take care of themselves and their families. Does your government have farming in the community or will the food be shipped from another area? Are goods and services readily accessible? People need to feel assured that provisions are available. If they do not, they will seek other places that will sustain them. A good example of this need is seen in the Sinagua Indian tribe of over 600 years ago. They left an intact village, including a 20-room five-story dwelling in what is now Camp Verde, Arizona. Experts believe they abandoned the village for no other reason than that they could not maintain enough supplies with the abilities and resources they had.

4. Law and order must be maintained. The apostle John wrote of the lack of order in a church in 3 John 1:9—"I wrote unto the church: but Diotrephes, who loveth to have the preeminence among them, receiveth us not. Wherefore, if I come, I will remember his deeds which he doeth, prating against us with malicious words: and not content therewith, neither doth he himself receive the brethren, and forbiddeth them that would, and casteth [them] out of the church." Diotrephes is an example of how even one person can cause great disorder. By his gossip and desire for being the "take charge" man, Diotrephes was actually causing a lot of problems in the growth of the **assembly**. The same principle is true in any organization or government: if there is not order, problems will arise. John was using Godly wisdom in pointing out the problem. Problems that are not addressed will grow larger until they become almost insurmountable. If a city is not organized, it will disintegrate. If a colony has no policing, it will soon be **decimated** by crime. Any government which does not take its law and order seriously will soon find itself in a precarious position. A number of Western mining towns that established a safe, orderly environment in the late 1800s were able to survive the closing of the mines, simply because people enjoyed living in a community with such privileges. Conversely, even a large city with a steady population can be in danger of collapsing if law and order become an insurmountable problem. An example of a city government learning the need to establish law and order is the city of East St. Louis, which experienced the travesty of near bankruptcy because of the loss of self-discipline and order.

5. The government should have a goal. "Where there is no vision, the people perish." (Proverbs 29:18). This is especially true when governing a group of people. If there are no set goals or challenges, where do the people aim? Is the group to grow, or merely to exist as they are? The dynamics of New York City's harbors made it a business area with a goal for international trade. It grew at an incredible rate. Jerusalem was and is a city of worship and still flourishes today. Many researchers believe that one of the main factors of Rome's decline was simply that there were no more goals.

Write the letter of the correct answer on the line.

1.1   One of the foundational rules for any government is to have a goal. What is the reference that tells

us "where there is no vision, the people perish?" _____

a.   Proverbs 3:5,6

b.   Psalm 119:1,2

c.   Proverbs 29:18

d.   Proverbs 28:1

e.   Psalm 1:4

Complete the following sentences.

1.2   A(n) _____ is a group of people settled in a particular area who carry the
same interests.

1.3   In a(n) _____ form of government, the goods and services are equally
shared, and the political power is distributed among the people.

1.4   There must be a final point of authority in a government. _____
of the Republic of Texas is a fine example of a leader who kept a government strong and active.

1.5   _____ and _____ should be provided daily to the population.

1.6   Measure must be taken to be safe. People settling in an area want to feel safe from outside attacks.
A previously mentioned example of a city which was founded as a fort with safety as a high priority

was the city of _____ .

1.7   Law and order must be maintained in order for a government to be strong. Problems must be
addressed. John gave us the example of dealing with disorder when he addressed the problem of

one man named _____ .

Match each word with its correct definition.

1.8   _____   decimate

1.9   _____   sustenance

1.10   _____   Sinagua Indian tribe

1.11   _____   Rome

1.12   _____   New York City

a. civilization that may have fallen due to lack of
goals

b. to reduce the amount in blocks or sizeable
amounts

c. settlement that relocated due to lack of
resources and sustenance

d. food and drink; necessary foods in order to
stay alive

e. grew due to the goals of increasing its international trade

Check the five basic essentials of leadership.

1.13 _____ The government should have a goal.

_____ At least one tenth of the citizens should be farmers.

_____ Raw materials should be stored.

_____ Safety is a priority.

_____ Leadership is needed.

_____ Law and order should be maintained.

_____ Production and sustenance should be provided daily.

_____ The fine arts should be shared among the populace.

_____ Higher education should be progressive.

Vocabulary

Study these words to enhance your learning success in this section.

aristocratic . . . . Belonging to nobility or privileged upper-class citizens.

assembly . . . . A body of Greek male citizens who would decide laws, enact government policies, and maintain authority.

city-state . . . . The ancient power structures; cities that were fortified into independent units of strength.

culture . . . . The belief, thoughts, and lifestyles of a particular community of people.

direct democracy . . . . The first name given to the Greek democracy.

lottery . . . . A form of choosing results or choosing men by the drawing of lots.

noble . . . . Lofty, financially well-to-do citizens who carried considerable power within the community.

right . . . . A moral or legal entitlement to have something because of law or God's direction.

tyrant . . . . Power-hungry militant who grabbed absolute control by force.

"Wicked men obey from fear; good men, from love."
— *Aristotle*

BEGINNING OF DEMOCRACY

The birth of democracy was in the Greek culture. If you had visited Greece a little over 400 years before Jesus walked through the streets of Jerusalem, you would have been able to witness the very first democracy known to man. You would find the governments different than most governments today; the Greek territories were divided into **city-states**, which meant that the cities and their outlying areas were independent from one another. Within these city-states the seeds of democracy were being planted. Within 100 years of your first visit to these regions, Aristotle and Plato would have been expounding the wisdom of government mainly by established laws. Greek democracy developed in Athens, and at first was called a **direct democracy**. Each male had a responsibility to serve on a permanent seat on the local assembly, deciding laws and government policies. The assembly set the rules and maintained authority. The democracy of Greek city-states was limited, women and slaves were not allowed to vote; yet, at that time it was a model of popular involvement.

Rivalries developed between the city-states, which can be considered a good thing. The fighting first occurred over land disputes between the two powers. Because of conflicts, the people of each city-state became politically involved and fiercely loyal to their government. The best known city-states were Athens and Sparta who had strong governments and powerful military forces. Sparta had a standing army, and Athens possessed a powerful navy. The city-states had a close-knit atmosphere similar to a family, and the governments were founded in their rough form around 700 B.C. At first, the city-states were ruled by an oligarchy, which was a small group of **aristocratic**-type men. Gradually, however, many male citizens were given the **right** to vote, serve on a jury, and hold public office.

A walk through Athens in 400 B.C. gives us a glimpse of the government of that area. We see a group of 500 men in session deliberating over a new law for the Athenians. These men were selected from a **lottery**, as were those serving on a jury. Though some of the poorer men could not leave work in order to serve in either office, the freedoms afforded to the citizens were highly valued and became a model for future governments.

Were the city-states always democracies? No, if we look back four more centuries we see that kings had ruled the city-states for centuries. They were concerned mostly with personal power and did little for the poor people who were barely surviving on what little they could farm from the land. **Nobles** overthrew most of the monarchs by 750 B.C. and opened the way for a new type of rule. These rich men owned much land and had vast power in the localized government. Unrest because of slavery and power-hungry nobles led to city-states being overthrown by leaders who wanted a change. These leaders were known as **tyrants**, because they had grabbed absolute control by force. Many of the tyrants achieved their original goals of getting farmland and jobs for the needy, but soon they too had power-hungry disputes. Oligarchies eventually replaced the tyrants, but then Athens made a political shift which helped change the history of government.

In 594 B.C. Solon was chosen as an Athenian statesman with reformation powers. Athens chose Solon to make laws to better assist the populace. Solon established a law which prohibited enslaving people in debt. He set up a strict code of law, and defined the duties of classes of people within the city-state. After he left office, his successor, Cleisthenes, presented a constitution in 508 B.C. This proposal opened up the voting rights to all free adult men. The assembly of 500 would include any citizen of Athens. Democracy was truly advancing toward the concept that rights and privileges should be provided for all citizens.

| Aristotle's mentor was Plato; Aristotle later tutored Alexander the Great.

Match each word with its correct definition.

1.14	_____	privileges
1.15	_____	rights
1.16	_____	tyrants
1.17	_____	lottery
1.18	_____	aristocratic
1.19	_____	assembly

a. being of nobility or of a privileged upper-class

b. a benefit enjoyed by a person out of grace or mercy. It is not owed to the person.

c. body of Greek male citizens who decide laws, enact government policies, set the rules, and maintain authority

d. things a person is entitled to because of law or God's direction

e. a form of choosing results or choosing men by the drawing of lots

f. power-hungry militants who grabbed absolute control by force

Check the statement that is NOT true.

1.20 _____ The Greek culture was actually the birth of democracy.

_____ "Direct democracy" was the first name given to the Greek democracy.

_____ Sparta's main strength was in its army.

_____ Athens's main strength was in its navy.

_____ Solon established a law which enslaved people in debt.

Complete the following statements.

1.21 The ancient power structures were cities fortified into independent units of strength called

_____ .

1.22 The proposal that opened up the voting rights to all free adult men in 508 B.C. was written by

_____ .

1.23 Nobles overthrew most of the monarchs by _____ .

1.24 In _____ B.C., Solon was chosen as an Athenian statesman with reformation powers.

Match each word with its correct definition.

1.25	_____	tyrants
1.26	_____	assembly
1.27	_____	Solon
1.28	_____	nobles
1.29	_____	oligarchy

a. lofty, financially well-to-do citizens who carried considerable power within the community

b. a small group of aristocratic-type rulers

c. set the rules and maintained authority within the city-state

d. power-hungry militants who grabbed absolute control by force

e. set up code of law and defined the duties of classes

Answer *true* **or** *false*.

1.30 _____ The democracy of Greek city-states was limited in that no women or slaves would be allowed to vote.

1.31 _____ The rivalries between the city-states had no redeeming value whatsoever.

1.32 _____ The law-making assembly in Athens consisted of a group of 1,000 free adult males.

1.33 _____ The beginnings of democracy were seen in Athens a little more that 400 years before Jesus walked the streets of Jerusalem.

Vocabulary

Study these words to enhance your learning success in this section.

accountability	Being answerable to others.
Concilium Plebis	The "common-people" assembly which helped give the citizens more political power.
empire	A dominating nation with extensive territories and a powerful ruler.
The Laws of the Twelve Tables	Guideline for citizens' behavior; a list of Roman customs about property and punishment.
mercenary	A soldier who is hired for service in a foreign country.
patrician	Member of Rome's richest and most important families who served on the Senate for life.
plebeian	The common person or lower-class citizen.
Roman Senate	One of the two houses of the early Roman republic.
republic	A country run by the elected representatives of its people.
tribune	Leader within the *Concilium Plebis*.

ANCIENT ROMAN GOVERNMENT

The beginnings of a people-involved government were seen in ancient Rome. Five hundred years before the time of Christ on earth, the Roman government was forming into what was to be a **republic**. In a republic, citizens have the freedom to vote for their leaders through elections. This afforded something new in the general thinking of governments: **accountability** to the people. There were two parts, or two houses, to the early Roman republic: the citizen assembly and the Senate. Two elected officials headed the two councils and served for one-year terms. The republic was established in 509 B.C. and lasted nearly 500 years.

What was the difference between the Greek and Roman governments? In early democratic-type governments, the wealthy still wanted to maintain control. It was no different in Rome. The difference between the Roman republic and the Greek democracy was that in Greece, all men were allowed to vote, but in Rome, only men with money and property could vote. Because of this, the common people needed to forge their way into the government. In the Senate, the most powerful part of the government, all senators were **patricians** (members of Rome's richest and most important families). To obtain political rights, **plebeians** (the common people) formed their own assembly, the *Concilium Plebis*, and named their leaders **tribunes**. Plebeians largely controlled the assembly and an active, cooperative government was formed.

Establishing peace and order gave Rome much-needed stability. The Romans' first code of law was established around 450 B.C. On 12 separate tablets, twelve legal experts wrote down a list of Roman customs about property and punishing people who did wrong. This code was called the **Laws of the Twelve Tables** (tablets on which the laws were inscribed) and at first its details of procedure were restricted to a body of patrician leaders. However, due to plebeian pressure, the Twelve Tables were put into writing around 450 B.C., making it more accessible to the common man for interpretation and understanding. By the end of the third century Roman law covered relations among Romans, dealings with foreigners, and eventually covered even magisterial law to strengthen and correct existing law. As the Roman **Empire** was increasing in dominance around 27 B.C., the law's development was taken over by the emperors, who added and revised freely. As the law grew more complex, the government literally trained jurists who could understand and correctly interpret the laws.

The stability of the law, the military, and financial standing of Rome kept it powerful. A number of enemies tried to overthrow the Roman republic, but they failed in their efforts. The Carthaginians, led by Hannibal, made a desperate and cunning attempt by marching elephants across the Alps. Even though Hannibal displayed brilliant strategies through the use of **mercenaries** and surprise attack, he could not sustain the advantage very long, and was forced to surrender. Rome also successfully battled the Celtics (now known as the British), the Etruscans, and the Samnites.

The Roman empire grew within and without. During the years of smoothly running governments, the Roman civilization grew. The Roman Empire was established in its strength around 27 B.C. Through the wisdom of its leaders, it had grown from a small republic into an empire that spanned three continents. Even as Roman power increased, Rome continued to be far-sighted in its planning. Its leaders took careful steps to maintain what they owned. The empire was divided into states that were ruled by a governor, who collected the taxes and sent the money back to Rome.

The early government of Rome demonstrates the importance of people's involvement in the decision-making process, by voting and serving in office. Rome showed how a republic could be run.

Complete the following statements.

1.34   To obtain political rights, plebeians formed their own assembly, _____ .

1.35   The Roman empire in its strength established itself around _____ B.C.

1.36   At first the details of procedure of the Twelve Tables were restricted to a body of

_____ leaders.

1.37   A dominating nation with extensive territories and a powerful ruler such as Rome's is known

as a(n) _____ .

1.38   The Romans' first code of law was established around _____ .

Check the statement that is TRUE.

1.39   _____   A mercenary is a soldier who is a former slave.

_____   The plebeians are upper-class citizens.

_____   The Romans' first code of law was established around 450 B.C.

_____   The republic lasted over 1000 years.

_____   The republic was also known as a socialist government.

Match each word with its correct definition.

1.40 _____ tribune

1.41 _____ Hannibal

1.42 _____ citizen assembly

1.43 _____ patricians

1.44 _____ governor

1.45 _____ accountable

a. members of Rome's richest and most important families

b. being answerable to others

c. leaders within the *Concilium Plebis*

d. a leader of the empire who collected the taxes
   and sent the money back to Rome

e. leader of the Carthaginians

f. one of two houses of the early Roman republic which consisted of regular middle-class
   male citizens of Rome

Place a check beside the enemies that the ancient Romans successfully battled.

1.46 _____ Samnites

_____ Etrusians

_____ Flavians

_____ Celtics

_____ Etruscans

_____ Carthaginians

Check the statements that are TRUE.

1.47 The difference between the Roman republic and the Greek democracy was that:

_____ In Rome, only men with money and property could vote.

_____ In the Greek Senate, even teenagers were allowed to participate.

_____ In the Roman government, no Greeks were allowed to serve.

_____ In Greece, all free men were allowed to vote.

_____ In the Roman Senate, the most powerful part of the government, all senators were
patricians.

_____ In the Greek government, retired soldiers were given automatic seats in the Senate.

Answer *true* **or** *false*.

1.48 _____ 500 years before the time of Christ on earth, the Roman government was forming what was to be a republic.

1.49 _____ The Roman House of Representatives was one of the two houses of the early Roman republic.

✓ **CHECK** _____
　　　　　　　　　Teacher　　　　　Date

↻ **Review the material in this section in preparation for the Self Test.** The Self Test will check your mastery of this particular section. The items missed on this Self Test will indicate specific areas where restudy is needed for mastery.

SELF TEST 1

Complete the following statements (each answer, 3 points).

1.01 One of the foundational rules for any government is to have a goal. _____ is the reference that tells us "where there is no vision, the people perish."

1.02 To obtain political rights, plebeians formed their own assembly, called _____ .

1.03 Another of the foundational rules for any government is that _____ and _____ should be provided daily to the population.

1.04 The beginnings of democracy were seen in _____ a little more than 400 years before Jesus walked the streets of Jerusalem.

1.05 A small group of aristocratic-type men in leadership is known as a(n) _____ .

1.06 *Nobles* overthrew most of the city-state monarchs by _____ .

1.07 "Where there is no _____ , the people perish." Proverbs 29:18

1.08 The Roman Empire in its strength established itself around _____ B.C.

1.09 The Romans' first code of law was established around _____ .

Answer *true* **or** *false* (each answer, 2 points).

1.010 _____ A socialist form of government is where the goods and services are equally shared, and the political power is distributed among the people.

1.011 _____ The Greek culture was the birth of democracy.

1.012 _____ The democracy of Greek city-states was limited in that no women or slaves were allowed to vote.

1.013 _____ The rivalries between the city-states had no redeeming value whatsoever.

1.014 _____ The law-making assembly in Athens consisted of a group of 1,000 free adult males.

1.015 _____ The Roman Republic was also a socialist government.

1.016 _____ At first, the details of procedure of the Twelve Tables were restricted to a body of patrician leaders.

Match each word with its correct meaning (each answer, 2 points).

1.017	_____	Pittsburgh	**a.** settlement that relocated due to lack of resources and sustenance
1.018	_____	Sam Houston	**b.** grew due to the goals of increasing its international trade
1.019	_____	colony	**c.** example of a city which was founded as a fort with safety in mind
1.020	_____	Sinagua Indian tribe	**d.** civilization that fell due to what many believe was a lack of goals
1.021	_____	Rome	**e.** a group of people settled in a particular area who have the same interests
1.022	_____	New York City	**f.** example of leader who kept a government strong and active

Check the five sentences that are the basic essentials of leadership (each answer, 2 points).

1.024 _____ Safety is a priority.

_____ Ethnic minorities should be ignored.

_____ Leadership is needed.

_____ Production and sustenance should be provided daily.

_____ Income tax should be immediately instituted.

_____ The government should have a goal.

_____ Law and order should be maintained.

Check the statement that is NOT TRUE (2 points).

1.024 _____ Sparta's main strength was in its navy.

_____ Athens's main strength was in its navy.

_____ Solon established a law which prohibited enslaving people in debt.

Match each word with its correct meaning (each answer, 2 points).

1.025	_____	tyrants	**a.** lofty, financially well-to-do citizens who carried much power within the community
1.026	_____	assembly	**b.** power-hungry militants who grabbed absolute control by force
1.027	_____	"direct democracy"	**c.** In 594 B.C. he was chosen as an Athenian statesman with reformation powers
1.028	_____	nobles	**d.** first name given to the Greek democracy
1.029	_____	Solon	**e.** set the rules and maintained authority within the city-state

Place a check beside the enemies that the ancient Romans DID NOT battle (each answer, 2 points).

1.030 _____ Samnites

_____ Etrusians

_____ Flavians

_____ Celtics

_____ Etruscans

_____ Carthaginians

Check the answer that is a TRUE statement (each answer, 2 points).

1.031 _____ A dominating nation with extensive territories and a powerful ruler such as Rome's is known as an empire.

_____ The plebeians are upper-class citizens.

_____ The Romans' first code of law was established around 200 B.C.

_____ The republic lasted over 1000 years.

Match each word with its correct definition (each answer, 2 points).

1.032 _____ tribune

1.033 _____ Hannibal

1.034 _____ citizen assembly

1.035 _____ patricians

1.036 _____ governor

1.037 _____ accountable

a. a leader of the empire who collected the taxes and sent the money back to Rome

b. one of two houses of the early Roman republic which consisted of regular middle-class male citizens of Rome

c. leader within the *Concilium Plebis*

d. being answerable to others

e. leader of the Carthaginians

f. members of Rome's richest and most important families

Check the statements which are TRUE (each answer, 2 points).

1.038 The difference between the Roman republic and the Greek democracy was that:

_____ The Roman House of Representatives was one of the two houses of the early Roman republic.

_____ In Rome, only men with money and property could vote.

_____ In Greece all free men were allowed to vote.

_____ In the Roman Senate, the most powerful part of the government, all senators were patricians.

_____ In the Greek government, retired soldiers were given automatic seats in the Senate.

Match each word with its correct definition (each answer, 2 points).

1.039 _____ decimate

1.040 _____ sustenance

1.041 _____ city-states

1.042 _____ Diotrephes

1.043 _____ Cleisthenes

a. John gave us the example of dealing with disorder when he addressed the problem of this man

b. to reduce the amount in blocks or sizeable amounts

c. wrote the proposal that opened up the voting right to all free adult men in 508 B.C. Athens

d. The ancient power structures were cities that were fortified into independent units of strength

e. food and drink, necessary foods in order to stay alive

$\frac{88}{110}$ **SCORE** _____   **CHECK** _____ _____

Teacher   Date

2. GOVERNMENTAL SYSTEMS

Section Objectives

Review these objectives. When you have completed this section, you should be able to:

4. Explain the concept of "feudalism" and its effect on people in the Middle Ages.

5. Describe a theocracy.

6. Describe a democracy.

Vocabulary

Study these words to enhance your learning success in this section.

aristocrat	Upper-class nobility.
feudal aid	Rights benefiting both lord and vassals, such as, vassals gave money at the marriage of the lord's eldest daughter.
feudalism	A system of cooperation among peoples which was basically an exchange of land for protection.
fief	The land granted to the vassal.
homage	A ceremony which bound the vassal to serve and protect the lord of the manor.
investiture	The vassal gives his allegiance and is given his rights to control the land but not have ownership of it.
knighthood	Able-bodied men who are hired by the vassal for the protection of the lord.
standing army	A group of soldiers ready to do battle.
subinfeudation	Breaking down an already-smaller portion of land in exchange for services and protection.
summons	A call to appear in court.
vassal	A man who would give protection to the lord in exchange for land.

FEUDALISM

The Middle Ages brought about the rise of a governmental system known as feudalism. Although feudalism was a highly decentralized system of authority, it was successful in meeting the needs of the medieval nobles. The primary political authority rested in local dukedoms and baronies and established a political system which had never been conceived before. Feudalism was an exchange of land for protection in which discipline, order, and a different type of currency set a new course in styles of government. Here was a type of government where no coin currency would have to change hands! An **aristocrat** would give vassals land in an agreement in which the vassals would then give military service to the lord. Only the upper echelon of society, such as noblemen, could take part in the feudal agreement. This system helped the rulers of the Middle Ages bring order to the nations, as lords granted fiefs (land) to those who vowed to give military protection to them. Feudalism started around A.D. 700 and was probably at its strongest from 900–1200 A.D. It served its purpose and was gone by the 15th century. It started in Northern Europe and spread throughout the continent, but was strongest in England. **Knighthood** was part of the lore of feudalism.

Let's consider a scenario to better understand the principles of feudalism. The scene is in England in the fictional area of Springbrook in the year 1100 A.D. The noble Robert of Springbrook needs to have protection over the vast lands that he owns. Robert knows of many good men who will be great and faithful leaders; so he calls them to become vassals in his manor. These men agree and an important ceremony known as **homage** sealed the commitment. The ceremony bound the **vassal** to serve and protect the lord of the manor, and the lord vowed to give honor to the vassal. It was a serious crime to break this pledge of commitment. Let's call one of the vassals Thomas the Vassal. An **investiture** ceremony followed the homage, where Thomas the Vassal is now accorded the land promised to him.

A vassal was given the rights to control the **fief**, but not to have ownership of it. Thomas now is given the right to receive the benefit of anything the land would produce, along with the right to hire workers. Anyone who lived in his fief would pay Thomas taxes and be subject to a court held by Thomas, should they break a rule of the fief. This could continue down through family lines even after Thomas died.

The relationship between the lord and vassals carried other financial responsibilities. In special rights called feudal aids, the lord had further financial protection. When the lord's eldest son was knighted or if his eldest daughter was married, the vassals would be required to provide money to him. Should the lord be in wartime and become captured in battle, the vassals were bound to provide ransom money for his release. On the other hand, the lord must not overtax his vassals unduly.

Robert of Springbrook calls on Thomas the Vassal and informs him that he should have his knights prepare to protect the kingdom. Thomas then hires knights to be suited up with armor and prepare for horse-mounted battle at short notice. Thomas agrees to give the knights a part of his fief in exchange to be part of his "**standing army.**" In exchange for the land, the knight agrees to be a sort of sub-vassal to Thomas. This agreement was known as **subinfeudation**. This layering of responsibility was for each level to be directly responsible to the level above them.

Knights had a valiant history throughout the feudalism period. They grew to form an association of knighthood called "orders." These knights vowed loyalty to the king and vassals for whom they fought. Realizing they would perform better as a group rather than as individuals, knights formed military organizations to defend their lord's land and property against the enemies. A medieval knight could also take religious vows to live as a monk in addition to his warrior status.

There were three steps to becoming a knight. When a boy turned 7, he was eligible to take the first step and become a page, where he joined the household of a knight or a nobleman in his particular region. The young page would then receive training on weaponry, etiquette, and the morals of knighthood. If the page passed the necessary requirements, he graduated to squire in his mid-teens. As a squire, he would personally serve the knight and undergo more intense training, eventually leading to being a mounted soldier who assisted his knight in battle. The squire training would continue for approximately five years until he was deemed eligible for

knighthood. The ceremony for knighthood could come from another knight, who would dress the squire in armor and dub him with a sword. The new knight would then follow a strict code of chivalry, including following the Christian faith. Knights were known for intense loyalty to their lords and severe justice to the ungodly.

The court system in feudalism is still seen today, as many of the parts of the lord's court have been carried down through the ages. If vassals had disputes among one another, the differences were brought to the lord's court. Today in our American courts we still carry the idea of one presiding authority, a judge and peers who will help in the decision making process, a jury. A vassal would answer a **summons** and obey the final decision of the court or lose his fief.

The vassal fiefdoms could become quite huge, as history demonstrates. King John of England ruled the land in the 1200s but in reality, he was a vassal to his lord, King Philip Augustus of France, for lands that were in France. King John refused some of the rulings of Philip, and war broke out between the factions. As a result, John lost some of his fiefs.

Match each word with its correct definition.

2.1 _____ aristocrat

2.2 _____ subinfeudation

2.3 _____ vassal

2.4 _____ feudalism

2.5 _____ summons

2.6 _____ standing army

a. a call to appear in court

b. a group of soldiers ready to do battle

c. upper-class nobility

d. breaking down an already-smaller portion of land in exchange for services and protection

e. a man who would give protection to the lord in exchange for land

f. a system of cooperation among peoples which was basically an exchange of land for protection

Complete the following statements.

2.7 An aristocrat would give vassals land in an agreement in which the vassals would then give _____ to the lord.

2.8 The lord wants some good men to become vassals in his manor. These men agree and an important ceremony known as a(n) _____ sealed the commitment.

2.9 In exchange for land, a knight agreed to be a sort of sub-vassal to a vassal. This agreement was known as _____ .

Write the letter of the correct answer on each blank.

2.10 Feudalism started around _____ .

    a. A.D. 600

    b. A.D. 700

    c. A.D. 1000

2.11 The system of cooperation known as feudalism ended around the _____ .

    a. 13th century

    b. 15th century

HISTORY & GEOGRAPHY 1204

LIFEPAC TEST

Name _____

Date _____

Score _____

105
131

Answer *true* **or** *false* (each answer, 2 points).

1. _____ A socialist form of government is where the goods and services are equally shared and the political power is distributed among the people.

2. _____ The democracy of Greek city-states was limited in that no women or slaves could vote.

3. _____ The law-making assembly in Athens consisted of a group of 1,000 free adult males.

4. _____ An aristocrat would give serfs land in an agreement in which the serfs would then give protection to the lord.

5. _____ The people of the United States voted for incumbent Republican Barack Obama over Democratic challenger Mitt Romney in the 2014 presidential election.

6. _____ Elected senators have six-year terms.

7. _____ The Federalist Papers were a defense for the brand new Declaration of Independence of the United States in a series of articles, written in 1787–1788.

8. _____ The Axis powers were made up of a coalition of countries that opposed the Allied powers in World War II.

9. _____ During World War II, Italy was an Axis power.

Complete the following statements (each answer, 3 points).

10. One of the foundational rules for any government is to have a goal. _____ is the reference that tells us "where there is no vision, the people perish."

11. _____ should be provided daily to the population.

12. A small group of aristocratic-type men in leadership is known as a(n) _____ .

13. The Roman Empire in its strength established itself around _____ B.C.

14. John gave us the example of dealing with disorder when he addressed the problem of

_____ .

15. First Samuel, chapter _____ , tells of the prophet Samuel's displeasure over the nation's desire for a monarchy.

16. "I will not rule over you, neither shall _____ rule over you, but the Lord shall rule over you" (Judges 8:23).

17. As we read in the Bible book of _____ , Moses was blessed—and punished— by God for his obedience or disobedience.

18. House representatives have _____ terms.

19. _____ could be the slogan of fascist governments.

20. In the fasces symbol, a bundle of elm or birch _____ were bound together by straps.

    The blade of a(n) _____ would protrude from the bundle, symbolizing unity and strength.

21. The atrocity of killing all of Europe's Jews by the Nazi government was known as the

    _____ by the Nazis.

22. William Penn said, "Those people who are not governed by God will be ruled by _____ ."

Match each term to its correct definition (each answer, 2 points).

23. _____ Sam Houston

24. _____ Sinagua Indian tribe

25. _____ New York City

26. _____ Assembly

27. _____ Athens

a. set the rules and maintained authority within the city-state

b. settlement that relocated due to lack of resources and sustenance

c. example of a leader who kept a government strong and active

d. grew due to the goals of increasing its international trade

e. main strength was its navy

Match each term with its correct definition (each answer, 2 points).

28. _____ tribune

29. _____ citizen assembly

30. _____ governor

31. _____ Roman Senate

32. _____ city-states

33. _____ A.D. 700

34. _____ summons

35. _____ standing army

a. one of the two houses of the early Roman republic which consisted of the rich and powerful

b. a group of soldiers ready to do battle

c. Feudalism started

d. a call to appear in court

e. a leader of the empire who collected the taxes and sent the money back to Rome

f. The ancient power structures which were cities that were fortified into independent units of strength

g. leaders within the *Concilium Plebis*

h. one of two houses of the Roman republic which consisted of regular middle-class male citizens of Rome

Match each term with its correct definition (each answer, 2 points).

36. _____ Muhammad

37. _____ Midianites

38. _____ fascist government

39. _____ direct democracies

40. _____ Nazi government

41. _____ concentration camps

42. _____ Nazi

a. Gideon refused to accept the kingship that the people offered him after his victory over these people

b. founder of Islam whose prophetic teachings became the basis of Islamic civilization

c. first word of the German title for the political National Socialist Workers' Party

d. had control of communications, military power, and social life

e. the form of government for the city-state of ancient Greece

f. detainment centers for many of Hitler's "undesirable" citizens

g. usually controlled by a dictator

Place a check on the correct answers (each answer, 2 points).

43. Select the enemies with which the ancient Romans *did* battle.

    a. _____ Samnites

    b. _____ Etrusians

    c. _____ Celts

    d. _____ Etruscans

    e. _____ Carthaginians

    f. _____ Flavians

Check the statement that is NOT TRUE (each answer, 2 points).

44. a. _____ Knights are able-bodied men who are hired by the vassal for the protection for the lord.

    b. _____ A vassal was given the rights to control the fief and to have ownership of it.

    c. _____ Feudal aid is where vassals would be ready to assist monetarily such as in giving ransom money in time of need.

    d. _____ A knight may serve a serf in exchange for horses.

    e. _____ Social reform is a call for change within a country with regard to education and culture, among other things.

45. a. _____ Massive fascist propaganda campaigns sweep the country in order to promote and allow freedom of religion.

    b. _____ In business, the fascists will control, focusing on high profits.

    c. _____ Social reform is a call for change within a country with regards to education and culture, among other things.

Check the answer that is a TRUE statement (each answer, 2 points).

46. a. _____ The fascist government encourages freedom of thought and expression.

b. _____ Fascists usually gain power after a country's economic collapse.

c. _____ Hitler led Germany into Nazism in the 1950s.

47. a. _____ In Nazi Germany, children were required to attend educational programs about Nazism.

b. _____ Hitler announced that Gypsies and Slavs were were exempt form the fascist "purging."

c. _____ Nazism is actually a form of democracy.

d. _____ Mussolini turned France into a Fascist government.

Check the statements which are TRUE (each answer, 2 points).

48. a. _____ Nazism and fascism have some similarities.

b. _____ Political, economic, and social, but not religious activities, are under the rule of a fascism government.

c. _____ Hitler ruled as a dictator and stirred the people to continue to be a "pure race."

d. _____ Hitler appealed to the continental glory that was due Europe.

e. _____ In a fascist government, worker strikes are never allowed.

Write the letter of the correct answer on the blank (each answer, 2 points).

49. Which of these men did *NOT* write the Federalist Papers? _____

a. John Jay

b. Alexander Hamilton

c. James Madison

d. Aaron Burr

Answer the following question (5 points).

50. Describe the parts of the medieval court system which are still used in our American court system today.

_____

_____

_____

_____

Check the statements that are TRUE.

2.12   a. _____   Feudalism is a system of cooperation among peoples which was basically an exchange of land for protection.

        b. _____   A vassal was given the rights to control the fief and to have ownership of it.

        c. _____   A summons is a call to appear in court.

        d. _____   When the vassal gave the lord his crops, it was known as feudal aids.

Check the statement that is NOT TRUE.

2.13   a. _____   A standing army is a group of soldiers ready to do battle.

        b. _____   King John of England in the 1200s was but a vassal himself.

        c. _____   Fiefs are upper-class nobility.

Match each word with its correct definition.

2.14   _____   knights   **a.** the land granted to the vassal

2.15   _____   feudal aid   **b.** layering of responsibility

2.16   _____   King John   **c.** able-bodied men who are hired by the vassal
                                                    for the protection of the lord

2.17   _____   fiefs
                                                d. vassals would be ready to assist monetarily
2.18   _____   subinfeudation   such as in giving ransom money in time of
                                                    need

                                                e. refused some of the rulings of Philip and war
                                                    broke out between the factions

Answer *true* **or** *false*.

2.19   _____   Feudalism started in Northern Europe and spread throughout the continent, but was strongest in England.

Describe the parts of the medieval court system which are still used in our American court system today.

2.20   _____

        _____

        _____

> "Have we not all one Father? Did not one God create us?"
> — *Malachi 2:10*

Vocabulary

Study these words to enhance your learning success in this section.

ascribing . . . . To give credit or honor to the source.

caliph. . . . . A supreme leader of the Islamic community and successor of the Prophet Muhammad.

commonwealth. A republic; a nation governed by the people.

Josephus . . . . A Jewish historian who lived shortly after Jesus walked the earth.

Muhammad . . . . Founder of Islam whose prophetic teachings became the basis of Islamic civilization.

Sharia . . . . The religious and moral principles of Islam.

submissive . . . . Meekly obedient and willing to surrender to the authority of another.

theocracy . . . . A government ruled by religious authority.

THEOCRACY

A theocracy is a nation under the rule of God. Theocracy is the constitution of a country in which God, or in some countries, a god, is regarded to be the sole authority and the laws of the nation are seen as divine commands. By comparison, democracy could be seen as a society under the rule of man. The leadership of a theocracy is not submissive to man's accountability, but looks to the direction and correction of God alone. Theocracy is a government where God himself is recognized as the head. The laws of the commonwealth are the commandments of God and the power of the church is greater than that of the state. There are no popular votes or referendums, the word is already set. In the case of Israel, you will remember in your Bible reading that there were no "polls" or "public opinion surveys" in order to sway God's thinking. God's dictates were the complete laws of the land.

We read of a theocratic government as Moses led the people out of Egypt from the hands of Pharaoh. Though Moses was the human leader, he was by no means in complete control. As we read in Exodus, Moses was blessed, and punished, by God because of his obedience or disobedience. The first time we read of the term "theocracy" is when we read the writings of the historian Josephus: "Our legislator [Moses] had no regard to any of these forms (of other governments), but he ordained our government to be what by a strained expression, may be termed a theocracy, by ascribing the power and authority to God, and by persuading all the people to have a regard to him as the author of all good things." (*Against Apion*, Book II, 16).

The Book of Judges tells us that Gideon refuses to accept the kingship that the people offered him after his victory over the Midianites. He expresses a severe statement of loyalty to God for a theocratic state, saying, "I will not rule over you, neither shall my son rule over you, but the Lord shall rule over you" (Judges 8: 23).

First Samuel, chapter 12, tells of the prophet Samuel's displeasure over the nation's desire for a monarchy instead of the theocracy which God had ordained. Samuel, in his speech to the people of Israel, reproaches them: "You said to me: Nay, but a king shall reign over us: whereas the Lord your God was your king. And at the call of the prophet the Lord sends thunder and rain as a sign of His displeasure, and you shall know and see that you yourselves have done a great evil in the sight of the Lord, in desiring a king over you."

There have been abuses of a theocracy. There have been feeble attempts to try to privately interpret God's leading outside of his Word and they ended in failure. Some examples are Jim Jones in Guyana, who led hundreds of people into mass suicide and Constantine of the Byzantine Empire, who required everyone to be "Christians," regardless of whether they gave their heart and life over to Jesus Christ as Savior.

A theocracy does not necessarily mean a nation that follows Jehovah God. For example, a **caliph** is the supreme leader of the Islamic community and successor of the Prophet Muhammad.

Under Muhammad, the Islamic state was a theocracy, with the Sharia, the religious and moral principles of Islam, as the law of the land. When Muhammad died in A.D. 632, a group of Islamic leaders elected Abu Bakr, the Prophet's father-in-law, to be the leader. Then Umar I became the second caliph in 634, and Islam expanded into Egypt, Syria, Iraq, and northern Mesopotamia. This theocracy had teachings that were not Biblical, nor did its followers follow the teachings of the Jehovah God.

| Gideon refuses the kingship, instead saying "the Lord shall rule over you."

Check the statement that is TRUE.

2.21 _____ The term "ascribing" is the art of carving sayings into rock.

_____ Theocracy is a rule of a nation under a series of commonwealths.

_____ Gideon was the first king of Israel who then abdicated because of the unrest which was building among the people.

_____ First Samuel, chapter 12, tells of the prophet Samuel's displeasure over the nation's desire for a monarchy.

_____ Eli was a high priest who later became the third king of Israel when he won a series of battles against the Philistines.

Answer *true* **or** *false*.

2.22 _____ Josephus was a Jewish historian who lived shortly after Jesus walked the earth.

2.23 _____ The leadership of a theocracy submits to man's accountability.

2.24 _____ Gideon refused to accept the kingship that the people offered him after his victory over the Midianites.

2.25 _____ Theocracy is always a government where Jehovah God himself is recognized as the head.

Complete the following statements.

2.26 The Biblical book of _____ tells us about the leadership of Gideon.

2.27 "I will not rule over you, neither shall _____ rule over you, but the Lord shall rule over you" (Judges 8:23)

2.28 As we read in the Bible book of _____ , Moses was blessed, and punished, by God because of his obedience or disobedience.

2.29 In the late 1970s, Jim Jones tried to institute a theocracy, but his abuse of the Bible only led the people of his community into _____ .

Match each word to its correct description.

2.30 _____ Muhammad

2.31 _____ Sharia

2.32 _____ caliph

a. the religious and moral principles of Islam

b. supreme leader of the Islamic community and successor of the Prophet Muhammad

c. founder of Islam whose prophetic teachings became the basis of Islamic civilization

"The Bible is the Book upon which this Republic rests."
— *Andrew Jackson, seventh president of the United States.*

Vocabulary

Study these words to enhance your learning success in this section.

Alexander Hamilton	One of three writers of the Federalist Papers, secretary of the treasury under George Washington.
electorate	The voting public.
The Federalist Papers	A defense of the brand new Constitution of the United States in a series of articles in 1787-1788.
indirect ballot	The elected representatives cast the vote in the place of the members they represent.
James Madison	One of three writers of the Federalist Papers, fourth president, and "the Father of the Constitution."
John Jay	One of three writers of the Federalist Papers and the first chief justice of the United States.
Prime Minister	Elected leader in a parliamentary democracy.
province	A territory of a nation.
representative	A member of a legislative power, elected by, and acting on behalf of the voters of his district.
term	An assigned period of time for an elected official.

DEMOCRACY

The people of the United States voted for incumbent Democrat Barack Obama over Republican challenger Mitt Romney in the 2012 presidential election. It was another coast-to-coast example of American democracy at work. Every time a citizen enters the voting booth at a local high school to vote on a town mayor, it's democracy in action. Every time a father makes a voting mark on the ballot for the next county sheriff, democracy is being exercised. Every time a college sophomore receives her voter's registration in the mail and heads to her precinct to vote, democracy is working. The democratic government in today's America still rolls on fervently, but it is a concept that goes back thousands of years.

Democracy is a great idea that started with the Greeks and Romans. The city-states of ancient Greece had citizens voting in direct democracies. A democracy is a system of politics in which the people of a nation actually rule by their voting power. They may choose a form of government which might be different from other countries in order to meet their particular needs, but it is still government by the people. In modern democracies, elected representatives are sent to the government seat to do the will of the people from their designated district. The representatives may even be replaced by the people according to the voting process called recall. Elected officials are directly accountable to the **electorate**.

Democratic nations may have different forms and styles of voting. For instance, each of Argentina's 23 provinces elects three senators to six-year **terms**. The United States has two houses of Congress, and the elected senators have six-year terms while House representatives have two-year terms. In 1991 Bangladesh created a parliamentary democracy, headed by a **Prime Minister**. Earlier that

| U.S. Constitution

year, a 300-member parliament was elected and 30 additional seats were subsequently filled by **indirect ballot**. Different nations exercise various forms of democracy. Nevertheless, the framework of democracy stays the same: the people have voting rights.

What makes a modern democracy so great: Four powerful pillars of democracy include the citizens' freedom, equality before the law, voting rights, and opportunity for education. Independent countries flock to the democratic system which, even with its flaws, still remains an immensely popular form of government, since there is a great margin for correction if the need arises.

One of the best American writings of democracy is the series of articles and essays known as The Federalist Papers (1787–1788). Written during the Revolutionary Era by the statesmen **John Jay**, **James Madison**, and **Alexander Hamilton**, the documents are a powerful display of the patriotism some of the American founding fathers had for their country's freedom. The papers defend the brand-new Constitution of the United States in a series of articles. The Federalist Papers present some of the most persuasive arguments for constitutional government ever written.

Despite its challenges and shortcomings, democracy still thrives today as strong as it did centuries ago. English journalist John Langdon-Davies made a bold public statement in 1936: "Democracy will be dead by 1950." We think he missed the mark, don't you?

Match each word with its correct definition.

2.33	_____	indirect ballot
2.34	_____	electorate
2.35	_____	province
2.36	_____	term
2.37	_____	prime minister
2.38	_____	representative

a. an assigned period of time for an elected official

b. elected leader in a parliamentary democracy

c. a territory of a nation

d. a member of a legislative power, elected by, and acting on behalf of the voters of his district

e. the elected representatives cast the vote in the place of the members they represent

f. the voting public

Complete the following statements.

2.39   The people of the United States voted for incumbent Democrat Barack Obama over Republican

challenger Mitt Romney in the _____ presidential election.

2.40   The city-states of ancient Greece had citizens voting in _____ .

2.41   In modern democracies, elected _____ are sent to the government

seat to do the will of the people from their designated _____ .

2.42   In _____ , Bangladesh created a parliamentary democracy, headed by a prime minister.

Answer *true* **or** *false*.

2.43   _____   An assigned period of time for an elected official is called a term.

2.44   _____   The Preamble was a defense for the brand-new Constitution of the United States in a series of articles, written in 1787–1788.

Choose the correct answer for the following statement.

2.45   An elected leader in a parliamentary democracy is called a _____ .

        a.   monarch

        b.   regent

        c.   caliph

        d.   prime minister

        e.   magistrate

Place a check on the correct answers.

2.46   The four powerful pillars of democracy are

_____   opportunity for education.

_____   taxation without representation.

_____   equality before the law.

_____   four representatives for each state or region.

_____   full access to public libraries.

_____   the citizens' freedom.

_____   voting rights.

Match each term with its correct definition.

2.47   _____   House representatives

2.48   _____   U.S. senators

2.49   _____   John Jay

2.50   _____   Alexander Hamilton

2.51   _____   James Madison

a. One of three writers of the Federalist Papers; one-time secretary of the treasury

b. have two-year terms

c. One of three writers of Federalist Papers, fourth president of the U.S; "the Father of the Constitution"

d. have six-year terms

e. One of three writers of the Federalist Papers; first chief justice of the United States

✔ **CHECK** _____ _____
                  Teacher   Date

↩ **Review the material in this section in preparation for the Self Test.** The Self Test will check your mastery of this particular section as well as your knowledge of the previous section.

SELF TEST 2

Answer *true* **or** *false* (each answer, 2 points).

2.01 _____ Under feudalism, an aristocrat would give vassals land in an agreement in which the vassals would then give protection to the lord.

2.02 _____ Feudalism started in Northern Europe and spread throughout the continent, but was strongest in Italy.

2.03 _____ First Samuel, chapter 12, tells of the prophet Samuel's displeasure over the nation's desire for a monarchy.

2.04 _____ The people of the United States voted for challenger Democrat Barack Obama over Republican incumbent Mitt Romney in the 2010 presidential election.

2.05 _____ The leadership of a theocracy is submissive to God's, or a god's, accountability.

2.06 _____ House representatives have two-year terms.

2.07 _____ Elected senators have four-year terms.

Match each word with its correct definition (each answer, 2 points).

2.08 _____ knights

2.09 _____ feudal-aid

2.010 _____ King John

2.011 _____ standing army

2.012 _____ homage

a. a group of soldiers ready to do battle

b. able-bodied men who are hired by the vassal for the protection of the lord

c. a ceremony where men become vassals in a lord's manor

d. ruled England in the 1200s

e. vassals would be ready to assist monetarily such as in giving ransom money in time of need

Check the statements that are NOT TRUE (each answer, 2 points).

2.013 _____ Feudalism is a system of cooperation among peoples which was basically an exchange of gold for protection.

_____ A vassal was given the rights to control the fief and to have ownership of it.

_____ A summons is a call to appear in court.

_____ A knight may serve a vassal in exchange for land.

Check the statement that is NOT TRUE (each answer, 2 points).

2.014 _____ A fief is the land granted to the vassal.

_____ King John of England was a vassal himself who refused some of the rulings of Ferdinand and war broke out between the factions.

_____ Subinfeudation is a layering of responsibility.

Write the letter of the correct answer in the blank (each answer, 2 points).

2.015   Feudalism started around _____ .

    a.   A.D. 600

    b.   A.D. 700

    c.   A.D. 1000

2.016   An elected leader in a parliamentary democracy is called a _____ .

    a.   monarch

    b.   regent

    c.   caliph

    d.   prime minister

    e.   magistrate

Complete the following statements (each answer, 3 points).

2.017   In exchange for land, a knight agrees to be a sort of sub-vassal to a vassal. This agreement was known as _____ .

2.018   The Bible book of _____ tells us about the leadership of Gideon.

2.019   "I will not rule over you, neither shall _____ rule over you, but the Lord shall rule over you" (Judges 8: 23).

2.020   Gideon refuses to accept the kingship that the people offered him after his victory over the _____ .

2.021   As we read in the Bible book of _____ , Moses was blessed, and punished, by God for his obedience or disobedience.

2.022   In the late 1970s, Jim Jones tried to institute a theocracy, but his abuse of the Bible only led the people of his community into _____ .

2.023   The three writers of the Federalist Papers were _____ , _____ , and _____ .

2.024   Four powerful pillars of democracy include: _____ , _____ , _____ , and _____ .

Match each word with its correct definition (each answer, 2 points).

2.025	_____	term
2.026	_____	Federalist Papers
2.027	_____	Bangladesh
2.028	_____	direct democracies
2.029	_____	Josephus
2.030	_____	Muhammad
2.031	_____	Sharia
2.032	_____	caliph

a. the form of voting for the city-states of ancient Greece

b. supreme leader of the Islamic community and successor of the Prophet Muhammad

c. a Jewish historian who lived just after Jesus walked the earth

d. founder of Islam whose prophetic teachings became the basis of Islamic civilization

e. the religious and moral principles of Islam

f. created a parliamentary democracy in 1991, headed by a prime minister

g. a defense of the brand-new Constitution of the United States in a series of articles, written in 1787–1788

h. an assigned period of time for an elected official

Check the statement that is TRUE (each answer, 2 points).

2.033 _____ The term "ascribing" is the work of writing on parchment.

_____ Theocracy is the rule of the people.

_____ A vassal could buy out his lord.

_____ The system of cooperation known as feudalism ended around the 15th century.

_____ King Richard was a king who later became a knight before going bankrupt.

Describe the parts of the medieval court system which are still used in our American court system today (5 points).

2.034 _____

_____

_____

_____

_____

75
94 **SCORE** _____   ✓ **CHECK** _____ _____
                                                Teacher   Date

3. DICTATORSHIP

Section Objectives

Review these objectives. When you have completed this section, you should be able to:

7. Describe fascism and give examples from history of fascist leaders and countries.

8. Describe and give a brief history of Nazism.

Vocabulary

Study these words to enhance your learning success in this section.

alliance	A close association of countries.
Axis	Coalition of countries that opposed the Allied powers in World War II.
dictator	A sole ruler of a nation; often cruel and abusive.
economic collapse	The financial panic and downfall of a country.
fasces	Rods bound by straps. The blade of an axe would protrude from the rods, symbolizing unity and strength.
fascism	Extreme totalitarian government run by a dictator and based on highly-emotional nationalism.
Mussolini	Italian Fascist party leader during World War II.
suppress	To subdue and limit the freedoms of people.

> **"The only stable state is the one in which all men are equal before the law."**
> — *Aristotle*

FASCISM

"This is the epitaph I want on my tomb: 'Here lies one of the most intelligent animals who ever appeared on the face of the earth.'" This is a quote of a man named Benito **Mussolini**. If you were to ask the families of the many thousands who were killed under the tragic regime of Mussolini, they would argue that Mussolini would definitely not be remembered for being one of the most intelligent people in history. Many of his decisions while in power as the leader of the Fascist party were barbaric and senseless. We will be studying **fascism** in this lesson, particularly the Fascist party led by Benito Mussolini.

Fascism is a form of government that demands complete control of its citizens in all areas of their lives. Political, economic, social, and even religious activities are under the rule of a fascist government, which is usually controlled by a **dictator**. "Ruling by strength" or "might makes right" could be the slogan of fascist governments. Though fascist governments allow private enterprise to function, personal liberties are severely curtailed.

Mussolini led the Italian Fascist party during World War II. One of the prime examples of a fascist government is that of Italy during the Second World War. In fact, the fascist leader Benito Mussolini coined the term "fascism." Economic conditions were poor in Italy following World War I, even though they had been on the winning side. Italians were upset because the peace treaties after the war had given them less territory than they had expected. The king of Italy was not able to relieve the nation's poverty, so the Fascist party made sweeping claims about reclaiming the rightful territories of the nation from the days of the Roman Empire. By 1922, the Fascist Party gained so much support from landowners and leaders of business and the military that it boldly maneuvered the king to make Benito Mussolini the prime minister. Upon receiving such power, Mussolini put the Fascists in control and made himself dictator. Having total control over education, communication, and even police, Mussolini abolished every other political party and began an iron grip reign over the populace. Mussolini led Italy into an **alliance** with Hitler's Germany during World War II and called themselves the **Axis** powers. The Allied powers of the U.S., Britain, and others overcame the Axis. Consequently, the Fascist government was overthrown and Italy surrendered.

Even the symbol for fascism denotes power. The **fasces** were a display of the government's strength in the time of the Roman Empire and were carried by the guards of the government officials. Fasces were made up of a bundle of elm or birch rods that were bound together by straps. The blade of an axe would protrude from the bundle of rods, symbolizing unity and strength. Though Mussolini started using the actual word fascism, the concept had been used as a powerful influence in many governments, including 1930s Hungary and Rumania as well as Napoleon's French empire in the early 1800s.

Fascists usually come to power by promising prestige or safety. The history of fascism usually shows the party gaining control of governments after an **economic collapse** or an outside threat. Though the party may even gain control by peaceful methods, the control they have is powerful and suppressing. No other political parties may have a share in running the country. Fascists may have a small group of leaders, but usually one leader-dictator will take complete control. Behind the cry for national glory, the dictator will assume control over the military and the educational system.

Even travel is often curtailed under fascism. Though a fascist country may become strong, it is at the expense of the individual. Personal liberties such as freedom of worship and cultural pursuits are ended. Massive propaganda campaigns sweep the country in order to promote the reasons for personal sacrifices. Children are required to attend educational programs that will not only teach them

the goals of the party, but also persuade them to completely support fascist policies.

In business, the fascists control focused on high profits. The government actually encourages private business, provided the businesses will serve the government in its functions. Strikes are strictly forbidden and insurrection may lead to imprisonment and even death. To stop work is felt to be equal with rebellion against the government.

Perhaps one of the most appalling traits of the fascist governments of history is an intolerance toward ethnic minorities. Whether Jews, Gypsies, Slavs or other minorities, fascists have hated these peoples and have allowed their persecution, even to the point of conducting their own deadly governmental "purging."

Hitler's Nazi Party carried many traits of the fascist beliefs. Hitler ruled as a dictator and suppressed any rebellion with brutal force. His hatred for Jews and other minorities led to the death of millions of innocents, while he stirred the German people to be a "pure race." Power was his byword and he appealed to the national glory that he said was due Germany.

| Benito Mussolini coined the term "fascism."

Match each word with its correct definition.

3.1 _____ alliance

3.2 _____ suppress

3.3 _____ Axis

3.4 _____ fasces

3.5 _____ dictator

3.6 _____ fascism

a. a sole ruler of a nation; often cruel and abusive

b. extreme totalitarian government run by a dictator and based on highly-emotional nationalism

c. elm or birch rods bound together by straps with the blade of an axe protruding, symbolizing unity and strength

d. coalition that opposed the Allied powers in World War II among the countries were Italy, Germany, and Japan

e. a close association of countries

f. subdue and limit the freedoms of people

Complete the following statements.

3.7 _____ could be the slogan of fascist governments.

3.8 One of the prime examples of a fascist government is that of the Italy during _____ .

3.9 In the fasces symbol, a bundle of elm or birch _____ , were bound together by straps.

The blade of a(n) _____ would protrude from the bundle, symbolizing unity and strength.

3.10 Personal liberties such as _____ and

_____ are ended under fascism.

Check the statement that is TRUE.

3.11 _____ Fascism is usually an agreement between three or more political parties.

_____ Fascists usually gain power after a country's economic collapse.

_____ Hitler led Italy into fascism in the 1930s.

Check the statements that are TRUE.

3.12 _____ The Axis powers were a coalition of countries that opposed the Allied powers in World War II.

_____ Political, economic, social, and even religious activities are controlled under the rule of a fascist government.

_____ A fascist government is usually controlled by a dictator.

Write the letter of the correct answer in the blank.

3.13   The fascist government actually encourages _____ .

   a.   public theater satires of the fascist thinking

   b.   private business, as long as the government is served

3.14   Fascist intolerance towards minorities culminates in _____ .

   a.   deadly governmental "purging"

   b.   a call for brotherhood

   c.   teachings in tolerance

Vocabulary

Study these words to enhance your learning success in this section.

chancellor . . . . A head of state in some forms of government.

concentration camp . . . . Detainment centers for Hitler's "undesirable" citizens, including those of the Jewish race.

Gestapo. . . . . Nazi secret police.

Great Depression . . . . Result of the stock market panic of the 1920s which brought on the 1930s worldwide economic slump.

inflation . . . . Financial instability brought on by continual increase in prices or continual decrease in purchasing power.

Nazism. . . . . A form of fascist government; probably the most extreme.

social reform . . . . A call for change within a country with regard to education and culture, among other things.

tyrannical government. . . . . Leadership taken and directed by force, often with bloodshed; an oppressive regime.

> **"We who lived in Concentration camps can remember the men who walked through the huts comforting others, giving away their last piece of bread. They may have been few in number, but they offer sufficient proof that everything can be taken from a man but one thing: the last of human freedoms—to choose one's attitude in any given set of circumstances—to choose one's own way."**
>
> *— Victor Frankl, speaking of the Nazi concentration camps*

NAZISM

The Nazi form of government was developed by dictator Adolph Hitler and was a catalyst in starting World War II. Also spelled **Nazism**, this form of government is actually a form of fascism. Personal liberties were restricted and minorities suffered as the one-party government grew in power. Of all the types of governments studied in this course, Nazism is probably the most extreme form of tyranny. It is puzzling to understand why people would want a government that hated democracy, incorporated mass murder, and controlled the press. Yet as you learn the steps leading up to Hitler's rise to power, you will see how people can grab for glory and stability whenever they have hope of little else. It is at times of great distress that **tyrannical governments** make their boldest moves.

The first opportunity for the Nazi movement came after World War I. Germany suffered a crushing defeat in 1918 and fell into extreme nationwide poverty. A democratic government did nothing to stem the flow of high **inflation** and unemployment that seemed to grow worse week by week. People grew desperate for change, and a man named Adolph Hitler gained control of a Munich political discussion group and renamed it the National Socialist Workers' Party, of which *Nazi* is the first word in German.

By the time of the Great Depression, the Nazi movement was growing into a national power. Hitler promised a great nation and the opportunity for Germany to increase its borders. He called for **social reform**, including the need to rid the country of inferior races which, he claimed, made the country impure. The global business crash known as the Great Depression turned the people to Nazism which was quite similar to fascism. It was similar to fascism in that the government had control of communications, military, and social life. Nazism, like fascism, allowed ownership of private property and some businesses as long as they served the Nazi movement.

Education and excitement helped empower the movement. Children were taught the Nazi doctrines of a superior race. The teaching was that the Germanic people along with other Northern Europeans were of a distinct and noble breed. Hitler went against the teachings of communism, socialism, and democracy, since they taught that people could be equal. Hitler wanted no part of being equal with

the Jewish, Slavic, or black races. National elections brought Adolph Hitler into political power in 1932. In the first month of 1933, Hitler became the prime minister of Germany, also known as **chancellor**.

A majority of the German citizenship welcomed Adolph Hitler into this new position of leadership. Surprising as it is now, few people of the country were surprised that the nation's Protestant church leaders were one of the most vocal in their support of Hitler's rise to power. Some churches went so far as to display Nazi flags in their church and upon their altars. A group of regional churches joined their congregations together in a centralized community known as the "German Christians," whose goal was to align with the Nazi way of thinking. One of the first acts of the "German Christian" movement was to apply the Nazi "Aryan Paragraph" law, which prohibited any people of Jewish heritage from holding a civil service, government, or ministerial position.

There was resistance to this new way of German thinking. Leading the rebellion against Nazism's anti-Semitic thinking was a young pastor by the name of Dietrich Bonhoeffer, who not only spent Sundays preaching against the Nazi doctrine, but also carried on many activities such as writing and lecturing throughout the week. While many Christians remained silent, Bonhoeffer became more vocal, even getting involved in political campaigns by urging people not to vote for those who had Nazi principles. He traveled to such places as London and Denmark, speaking to congregations and conventions alike. Bonhoeffer's efforts included helping

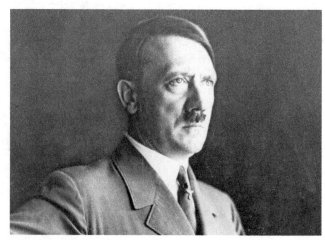

| Adolph Hitler

create organizations and seminaries for those who did not wish to follow Nazism.

Despite the pockets of opposition, Hitler continued to rise in power and popularity. He established the power base he needed and moved the nation toward a totalitarian state, in which there was no opposition to him. Secret police known as the **Gestapo** would detain anyone suspected of opposing the Nazi thinking. Concentration camps were set up for those who opposed him, but Jews and other minorities were also held in the camps. With the growth of Germany's power, the "final solution" of

killing all of Europe's Jews went into effect. The numbers reported vary, but there is no doubt that many millions of the Jewish race were exterminated.

As brutal and unappealing as Nazism appears, it is important that we understand bad government, so that we may remember how to maintain good government. As Nazis performed atrocious acts which were in conflict with God's laws, it is wise for us to remember the words of William Penn: "Those people who are not governed by God will be ruled by tyrants."

Match each word with its correct definition.

3.15 _____ concentration camps

3.16 _____ Nazism

3.17 _____ tyrannical government

3.18 _____ inflation

3.19 _____ social reform

3.20 _____ first month of 1933

3.21 _____ Gestapo

3.22 _____ chancellor

3.23 _____ "final solution"

3.24 _____ Great Depression

a. a call for change within a country with regard to education and culture, among other things

b. Hitler became the prime minister

c. detainment centers for many of Hitler's "undesirable" citizens, including those of the Jewish race, multitudes were killed while imprisoned in these centers

d. leadership taken and directed by force, often with bloodshed, an oppressive regime

e. financial instability which could be brought on either by continual increase in prices or continual decrease in the purchasing power of money

f. a form of fascist government; probably the most extreme form of tyranny

g. Result of the stock market panic of the late 1920s

h. Nazi secret police

i. a head of state in some forms of government

j. killing all of Europe's Jews by the Nazi government

Answer *true* **or** *false*.

3.25 _____ Nazism is a form of fascist government; probably the most tolerant form of democracies.

3.26 _____ Nazism is actually a form of fascism.

3.27 _____ The first opportunity for the Nazi movement came after World War II.

3.28 _____ *Nazi* is the first word of the German title for the political National Socialist Workers' Party.

3.29 _____ The Nazi government had control of communications, military power and social life.

Complete the following statements.

3.30 "Those people who are not governed by God will be ruled by tyrants," is a quote from

_____ .

3.31 Detainment centers for many of Hitler's "undesirable" citizens, including those of the Jewish race

were called _____ . Multitudes were killed while imprisoned in these centers.

✓ **CHECK** _____ _____
                              Teacher   Date

↺ **Before you take this last Self Test, you may want to do one or more of these self checks.**

1. _____ Read the objectives. Determine if you can do them.
2. _____ Restudy the material related to any objectives that you cannot do.
3. _____ Use the **SQ3R** study procedure to review the material:
   a. **S**can the sections.
   b. **Q**uestion yourself again (review the questions you wrote initially).
   c. **R**ead to answer your questions.
   d. **R**ecite the answers to yourself.
   e. **R**eview areas you did not understand.
4. _____ Review all vocabulary, activities, and Self Tests, writing a correct answer for every wrong answer.

SELF TEST 3

Answer *true* **or** *false* (each answer, 2 points).

3.01 _____ A fascist government is usually controlled by a dictator.

3.02 _____ Fascism is usually an agreement between three or more political parties.

3.03 _____ Nazism is actually a form of fascism.

3.04 _____ The first opportunity for the Nazi movement came after World War I.

3.05 _____ Social reform is a call for change within a country with regard to education and culture, among other things.

3.06 _____ Nazi secret police were known as the Gestapo.

Match each word to its correct definition (each answer, 2 points).

3.07 _____ Nazi government

3.08 _____ William Penn

3.09 _____ concentration camps

3.010 _____ Great Depression

3.011 _____ *Nazi*

a. result of the stock market panic of the late 1920s

b. first word of the German title for the political National Socialist Workers' Party

c. had control of communications, military power, and social life

d. "Those people who are not governed by God will be ruled by tyrants."

e. detainment centers for many of Hitler's "undesirable" citizens

Complete the following statements (each answer, 3 points).

3.012 _____ could be the slogan of fascist governments.

3.013 One of the prime examples of a fascist government is that of Italy during _____ .

3.014 Fasces were a bundle of elm or birch _____ bound together by straps. The blade of an axe would protrude from the bundle, symbolizing unity and strength.

3.015 Personal liberties such as _____ and

_____ are ended under fascism.

3.016 The atrocity of killing all of Europe's Jews by the Nazi governments was known as the

_____ by the Nazis.

3.017 The head of state in some forms of government is known as a _____ .

Check the statement that is TRUE (each answer, 2 points).

3.018 _____ The fascist government discourages private business.

_____ Fascists usually gain power after a country's economic collapse.

_____ Hitler led Italy into fascism in the 1930s.

Check the statements that are TRUE (each answer, 2 points).

3.019 _____ The Axis powers were made up of a coalition of countries that opposed the Allied powers in World War II.

_____ Political, economic, and social, but not religious activities, are under the rule of a fascism government.

_____ Strikes are allowed only in cases of national concern under fascism.

_____ Hitler's Nazi Party carried many traits of the fascist beliefs.

Complete the following statement (2 points).

3.020 Hitler ruled as a dictator and _____ .

a. appealed to the continental glory that was due Europe

b. announced that Gypsies and Slavs were exempt from the fascist "purging"

c. stirred the people to continue to be a "pure race"

d. allowed travel through Europe

Check the statement that is NOT TRUE (each answer, 2 points).

3.021 _____ Massive fascist propaganda campaigns sweep the country in order to promote freedom of religion.

_____ In business, the fascists will control focusing on high profits.

_____ Children are required to attend educational programs about Nazism.

$\frac{42}{53}$ **SCORE** _____ ✓ **CHECK** _____ _____
Teacher   Date

↺ **Before taking the LIFEPAC Test, you may want to do one or more of these self checks.**

1. _____ Read the objectives. Determine if you can do them.
2. _____ Restudy the material related to any objectives that you cannot do.
3. _____ Use the **SQ3R** study procedure to review the material.
4. _____ Review activities, Self Tests, and LIFEPAC vocabulary words.
5. _____ Restudy areas of weakness indicated by the last Self Test.

NOTES